Vampire Game

JUDAL

Translator - Ikoi Hiroe
English Adaptation - Jason Deitrich
Associate Editor - Tim Beedle
Retouch and Lettering - Jennifer Nunn-Iwai
Cover Layout - Anna Kernbaum

Editor - Luis Reyes
Managing Editor - Jill Freshney
Production Coordinator - Antonio DePietro
Production Manager - Jennifer Miller, Mutsumi Miyazaki
Art Director - Matt Alford
Editorial Director - Jeremy Ross
VP of Production - Ron Klamert
President & C.O.O. - John Parker
Publisher & C.E.O. - Stuart Levy

Email: editor@TOKYOPOP.com

Come visit us online at www.TOKYOPOP.com

A  Manga

TOKYOPOP Inc.
5900 Wilshire Blvd. Suite 2000
Los Angeles, CA 90036

Vampire Game vol. 5

ISBN: 1-59182-557-1

First TOKYOPOP printing: March 2004

10 9 8 7 6 5 4 3 2 1

Printed in the USA

VAMPIRE GAME

Volume 5

by

JUDAL

Los Angeles • Tokyo • London

VAMPIRE GAME

The Story Thus Far...

This is the tale of the Vampire King Duzell and his quest for revenge against the good King Phelios, a valiant warrior who slew the vampire a century ago. Now Duzell has returned, reincarnated as a feline foe to deliver woe to...well, that's the problem. Who is the reincarnation of King Phelios?

Duzell and Princess Ishtar have journeyed to Ci Xeneth, the home of Ishtar's Uncle Jened. Between his obsession with Ruelles, his collection of monsters in the basement, and his lust for the throne of Pheliosta, Jened is one of the most repulsive rulers to ever see sovereignty. His desire to both marry and murder his niece is recognized, as is the assumption that he probably won't do it in that order. However, one good thing has come from Jened–his daughter Falan. As pure as her father is putrid, she's adored by Ishtar and beloved by the people of Ci Xeneth.

While neither Jened nor Falan seem like the reborn Phelios, the fact remains that they could be. Of course, to know for sure, Duzell must sample their blood, which unfortunately means getting close to Jened. Deciding to delve as deep undercover as the shallow Ishtar can bear, they befriend the palace guard. After all, who's likely to harbor more resentment towards Jened than those on his payroll?

スタ
スタ
スタ
LIEU-TENANT!
THAT WAS A BIT HARSH, DON'T YOU THINK?!
THOSE MEN WERE MASSACRED, MUTILATED AND STRUNG-UP IN THE MARKET! WHAT THE DEVIL ARE WE TURNING INTO?
THOSE MEN HAD FAMILIES!

CALM DOWN, ROY.
AS FAR AS I'M CONCERNED, THOSE BANDITS GOT WHAT THEY DESERVED. AT LEAST THIS WAY THEY'RE CONTRIBUTING SOMETHING TO SOCIETY.
THOSE MEN WERE THIEVES AND MURDERERS. YOU SPEAK OF FAMILIES...
WHAT ABOUT THE FAMILIES OF THE MEN THEY KILLED?
LET THEM REMIND THE PEOPLE OF CI XENETH THAT LORD JENED WILL NOT TOLERATE LAWBREAKERS.
OUR JOB ISN'T TO TERRIFY PEOPLE!! WE'RE SUPPOSED TO KEEP THEM FROM LIVING IN FEAR!!
HI, ILLSAIDE!

COME ON, BE A NICE KITTY.
ALL RIGHT! ALL RIGHT!
I ACCEPT YOUR OFFER.
OFFER? WHAT OFFER?

THIS BOY'S SWORD HAD BETTER BE QUICKER THAN HIS WITS.

YOU KNOW ... THE "I WANT YOU TO BE MY MAN" OFFER.

OH YEAH! UM...VERY GOOD. THANK YOU.
DID HE JUST BLUSH?
AND WHAT'S WITH THAT SMILE?
YOU'RE THE MAN, CAPTAIN!
CONGRAT-ULATIONS!

I'M NOT VERY GOOD AT THIS KIND OF THING, SO I DON'T REALLY KNOW WHAT TO SAY. BUT I'M GLAD YOU SAID YES. THANK YOU.

WHAT KIND OF THING?
I WAS EXPECTING, "WELCOME TO THE TEAM..."
OR MAYBE, "GLAD TO HAVE YOU ABOARD..."
わい
わい
わい

BUT THEY'RE ACTING LIKE A BUNCH OF SCHOOLGIRLS.
WHAT THE HELL'S GOING ON?

OH, HEY! I JUST REALIZED THAT I DON'T EVEN KNOW YOUR NAME!
YOURS OR YOUR BROTHER'S.
OH, I'M--

THAT'S DU.
I'M ISHTA.
INTERESTING NAMES. DID YOU PICK THEM YOUR-SELVES?
NOPE! MY FATHER NAMED US AFTER THE FUTURE QUEEN OF PHELIOSTA AND THE LEGENDARY VAMPIRE KING! AND IF YOU THINK THAT'S WEIRD, YOU SHOULD HEAR WHAT HE NAMED OUR SISTER!
ANYHOW, WE GO BY DU AND ISHTA.
Although sometimes I call him Duzie...
NOTE TO SELF, STRANGLE "ISHTA" AS SOON AS WE GET HOME.

SO, YOU'RE DU.
GIVE ME YOUR HAND.

GORGEN ...
CAN YOU HANDLE THE LILKE WITHOUT ME? I'M GOING TO BE A LITTLE... BUSY.
OF COURSE, MY CAPTAIN ...

HMM... MAYBE I SHOULD'VE TOLD DUZELL.
OH WELL, TOO LATE NOW! I'M SURE HE'LL BE FINE. HE DOES HAVE CLAWS, AFTER ALL.

THEN AGAIN, ILLSAIDE MIGHT ACTUALLY LIKE THAT...
ISHTA...
I UNDERSTAND YOU CAN USE HOLY MAGIC. WE'D BE HONORED IF YOU WOULD JOIN US.
WE'RE HUNTING LILKE.
IT SHOULD BE FUN.
A CHANCE TO REVEL IN OUR MANLI-NESS.
LILKE?

WHERE HAVE I HEARD THAT WORD BEFORE?
HMMMM...
PRIN-CESS!
PRINCESS FALAN!

YES?
?
THERE YOU ARE! WHAT WERE YOU LOOKING AT DOWN THERE?
NO ONE...
I MEAN, NOTHING SPECIAL.
IF YOU INSIST, MILADY.

YOUR FATHER IS WAITING FOR YOU AT THE BREAKFAST TABLE.
AND THOSE FABRICS HE ORDERED ARRIVED THIS MORNING! THE ONES FOR YOUR NEW DRESSES!
YOU'LL HAVE THE PRETTIEST GOWNS AT THE HOLIDAY FESTIVALS!
I'VE NEVER SEEN ANYTHING LIKE THEM!
YOU MUST BE THE HAPPIEST GIRL IN THE WORLD!

WAIT A SECOND!
YOU WANT ME TO HELP YOU KILL THAT?!
SHE'S SO BEAUTIFUL! AND SHE HASN'T HURT ANYBODY.
I COULD NEVER DO IT...
I'M SORRY, BUT YOU'RE ON YOUR OWN!

SHHH!

AAARGH!
ROY!
SHE'S SPOTTED US!
ATTACK !!

REMEMBER! WE NEED HER ALIVE!
SUBDUE HER, BUT DON'T KILL HER!!
THEY'RE TRYING TO CAPTURE IT?
WHY?
SOME-THING'S WRONG...
I'VE NEVER SEEN A... LILKE DO THAT...
I CAN'T SEE... ISHTA? I CAN'T...
ホトホト

SHHH! YOU NEED TO STAY CALM.
I TURNED THE MAN INTO A WOMAN.
ONLY PROBLEM IS THAT THE LAST TIME I TRIED CASTING IT...
WE NEED A HEALING SPELL!
WAIT! I KNOW A HEALING SPELL...
LORD JENED... NEEDS THE LILKE...
TO MAKE A... RUELLE OF TRANSPORT-ATION. H-HE ASKED US... TO CATCH ONE...
W-WE'VE BEEN T-TRAINING... FOR THIS HUNT FOR... WEEKS...
BUT NO ONE...EVER SAID THEY... COULD DO THAT!

A RUELLE OF TRANS-PORTATION?
LIKE MY RING?

BY THE WAY...
MY LIFE HAS GOTTEN SO WEIRD.
...WHEN IT'S CONVENIENT, I'D LIKE TO MEET LORD JENED.
SO I CAN BITE HIM AND SEE IF HE'S THE REINCARNATION OF PHELIOS.
SURE, NO PROBLEM.

I'D ALSO LIKE TO MEET PRINCESS FALAN.

WHEN SHE'S GOT SOME FREE TIME, OF COURSE.

I THINK I'M THE FIRST VAMPIRE IN HISTORY TO FEEL EMBARRASSED. IT DOESN'T SUIT US...

I wonder what Princess Falan will taste like...

DU, WHAT EVER HAPPENS, I JUST WANT YOU TO KNOW...
...I'D GIVE MY LIFE TO PROTECT YOU.
NOT THIS AGAIN...
LOOK, BUB, I SLAUGHTERED HALF THE FREE WORLD. I REALLY DON'T NEED YOU TO PROTECT ME.

吸血遊戯
シー・ゼネス
東領篇
Act.4

わあああああ！
ボタ
ボタ

THIS CAN'T BE HAPPENING!

I'VE STUDIED MAGIC SINCE I COULD TALK. BUT WHEN I REALLY NEED IT, I'M COMPLETELY USELESS!! SHOULD'VE PAID MORE ATTENTION TO YUJINN.

ROY!!

WAIT...

PLEASE, SIDIA!
I NEED TO HELP ROY!

HMM...WELL, THAT'S INTERESTING.

YOU'RE THE LAST PERSON I EXPECTED TO MEET HERE...
...PRINCESS ISHTAR.

...HIS EYE WAS COMPLETELY HANGING OUT OF THE SOCKET! HE WASN'T HEALED COMPLETELY, BUT...
...WHEN HE GOT BACK TO THE BARRACKS, THE HEALER SAID HE COULD PATCH HIM UP GOOD AS NEW!
I DID GOOD, HUH?!
YOU DID GOOD?
YOU COULD HAVE KILLED HIM!
HOW COULD YOU EVEN THINK OF CASTING A SPELL LIKE THAT?! REMEMBER YOUR MAGIC TEST?! JUST ONE WRONG INTONATION AND "WINGS OF MERCY" BECOMES A TRANSFORMATION SPELL!
YOU'RE DAMN LUCKY YOU DIDN'T TURN HIM INTO A PRINCESS!
LOOK, YOU CAN PRACTICE ALL YOU WANT ON THESE HUMANS, BUT DON'T YOU EVER TRY CASTING THAT ON ME! GOT IT?!

CAN I SAY SOME-THING, DUZIE?
WHAT?
I DIDN'T CAST THE SPELL.
HUH?
I KNEW I'D NEVER GET "WINGS OF MERCY" RIGHT, AND I COULDN'T REMEMBER HOW "SUCCORELLE" STARTS.
THAT ONE ALWAYS CONFUSES ME.
SO I WAS GOING TO USE "BURN BEGONE"--I KNOW THAT ONE FOR SURE--AND SEE HOW MUCH SIDIA BOOSTED ITS POWER!
"BURN BEGONE"?!
THEY TEACH THAT SPELL TO SCHOOLCHILDREN!

THAT POOR BASTARD...
HE MUST HAVE REALLY DONE SOMETHING WRONG IN HIS LAST LIFE.
BUT IT WAS LIKE...
...SIDIA...
...KNEW WHAT I NEEDED...
...AND CAST A HEALING SPELL THROUGH ME!
FUNNY, HUH?

COME ON!
SIDIA ISN'T ALIVE! IT COULDN'T HAVE KNOWN YOU NEEDED HELP!
WELL, IT DID.
HE'S RIGHT. I THINK...
STILL, I CAN'T HELP THINKING ABOUT THAT POOR LILKE.
ROY SAID THEY WERE GOING TO USE IT TO CREATE A MAGIC RING. THEY WANTED IT ALIVE...

ONLY AN ARCHMAGE CAN CRAFT A RUELLE, BUT THEY DON'T EXACTLY GROW ON TREES. I WONDER IF UNCLE JENED FOUND ONE.
I SHOULD PROBABLY FIND OUT MORE BEFORE I TELL DUZELL.
UNLESS...
NAH, COULDN'T BE.
SO, DUZIE, HOW'D IT GO ANYWAY?

YOU KNOW, WITH ILLSAIDE.
I DON'T THINK...
...GETTING CLOSE TO YOUR UNCLE AND COUSIN IS GOING TO BE A PROBLEM.
BUT THINGS ARE GETTING KIND OF STRANGE.
STRANGE?
ILLSAIDE SAID HE WAS IN LOVE WITH ME.
HE SAID WHAT?!

HE, UH... ASKED ME TO BE HIS BOYFRIEND.

HE'S INTRODUCING ME TO YOUR UNCLE TONIGHT.

THERE'S SOMETHING I DON'T GET, THOUGH. ISN'T IT A BIT WEIRD TO SHOW OFF YOUR...BOY TOY...TO YOUR ARMY BUDDIES? I MEAN, A GIRLFRIEND I COULD UNDERSTAND, BUT A BOYFRIEND?

YOU SAID I WAS YOUR SISTER ?!

ニコッ

I HEARD MY KNIGHTS HAD SOME PROBLEMS WITH THIS CREATURE. THEY TRY, YOU KNOW?
SHE'S BEAUTIFUL, DIAAGE!

BUT YOU SHOULD NEVER SEND A SOLDIER TO DO A SORCERER'S JOB, RIGHT?!

MY LORD ...
THE CREATURE WAS ENCHANTED.

SIR GORGEN AND HIS MEN COULD NOT HAVE CAPTURED HER WITHOUT HELP.

NO, CAPTAIN ILLSAIDE WASN'T...

THE CAPTAIN WAS--

ANSWER ME!
WHAT THE HELL WAS SO IMPORTANT ...
...THAT YOU WOULD DELIBERATELY DEFY ME?!!

I WAS LYING IN A MEADOW... WITH A WOMAN.
A WOMAN?
WHAT? ARE YOU TELLING ME YOU HAVE A GIRL-FRIEND?
I'M IN LOVE.
I THINK I'VE FOUND MY SOUL MATE.

I NEVER WOULD HAVE THOUGHT ...
...THAT I'D HEAR THOSE BEAUTIFUL WORDS COME OUT OF YOUR MOUTH!
くしゃ
I SUPPOSE TRUE LOVE IS MORE IMPORTANT THAN A LILKE OR TWO! RIGHT, GENTLEMEN?
SO...

...WHEN DO I GET TO MEET THE LUCKY LADY?
SAY, WHY DON'T YOU BRING HER BY TONIGHT FOR DINNER?
I'LL HAVE FALAN JOIN US!

DUZIE... DON'T BE MAD AT ME!
EASE ?
PRETTY PLEASE?
C'MON, YOU'RE UNDERCOVER, REMEMBER?
THINK OF IT AS A DISGUISE! BESIDES, ILLSAIDE LIKES YOU, AND HE'S GOING TO GET YOU CLOSE TO UNCLE JENED.
YOUR MISSION IS GOING GREAT! NOW LET'S GO GET YOU ALL PRETTIED UP!
PRINCESS, IF YOU INSIST...
...ON HOOKING ME UP WITH MEN...
ST AKE URE EY'RE MY TYPE!
YOU EXPECT A VAMPIRE KING TO DATE KNIGHTS AND PRINCES? COME ON!
ISHTA!!
DU!

ROY!
YOU'RE OUT OF BED?
THE HEALER SAID YOU SHOULD REST FOR A COUPLE OF DAYS!
I'M FINE.
SIR DIAAGE, THE MAGICIAN THAT HELPED... HE'S BEEN TREATING ME PERSONALLY!
I'VE NEVER FELT THIS GOOD!
DIAAGE?
OH, YEAH! THE SCARY-LOOKING GUY.
YEAH!
LORD JENED JUST MADE HIM HIS HIGH SORCERER. THEY SAY HE'S AN ARCHMAGE!

AN ARCH-MAGE? REALLY?
DIAAGE? HMM...
I KNOW A WOMAN WITH THAT NAME. BUT IT CAN'T BE HER. THAT WAS SO LONG AGO...
Nope, this was definitely a dude.
He has hairy ears, man.
ANYHOW, SIR DIAAGE SAID THAT THE LILKE WE CAUGHT...
...WAS ENCHANTED.
THAT'S HOW IT WAS ABLE TO BEAT OUR BUTTS SO BAD.

WAIT! HOW WAS IT ENCHANTED?
I DON'T REALLY UNDERSTAND IT, BUT SIR DIAAGE SAID IT'S KIND OF LIKE THE "GUARDIAN" SPELL THAT VAMPIRES USE.
HE THINKS IT MIGHT BE MERARIM SABOTEURS. IT WOULDN'T SURPRISE ME CONSIDERING WHAT JENED DID TO THEIR QUEEN...
AT ANY RATE, KEEP YOUR EYES OPEN.
THE "GUARDIAN"!
I'M REALLY GETTING SICK OF THAT SPELL.
I WONDER...

COULD THAT VAMPIRE FROM LA NAAN HAVE SOMETHING TO DO WITH THIS? DOUBTFUL...
STILL, THAT'S NO HICKEY OUR BOY ROY IS SPORTING ON HIS NECK.
DU, YOU HAVE A ROYAL SUMMONS!
LORD JENED WOULD LIKE FOR YOU AND THE CAPTAIN TO JOIN HIM FOR DINNER TONIGHT.
OH... I ALMOST FORGOT!
OH, YEAH! EVEN AS A GIRL, I'M STILL THE MAN!

UM... OKAY, NOT CERTAIN OF WHAT YOU'RE... IT'S NO MATTER. FORMAL COURT DRESS IS REQUESTED.
DID YOU SAY FORMAL COURT DRESS?
ALL RIGHT, PRINCESS, I DRAW THE LINE AT WEARING A DRESS. YOU'LL HAVE TO SWITCH PLACES WITH ME.
?

La Naan Castle
ISHTAR'S GONE?!
....
I WAS HOPING SHE MIGHT'VE COME HERE.

AFTER MORE THAN TEN YEARS OF LOOKING FOR HER...
...UNDER BEDS, IN CLOSETS, UP IN THE HAYLOFTS AND OUT IN THE MEADOWS...
...MY GUT TOLD ME SHE WOULD COME BACK TO LA NAAN. HER MEMORY SPAN IS ONLY SO LONG...
Darres' imagination
HEY! I CAN USE THE RING TO GO TO THE MOUNTAINS AND PICK MUSHROOMS!
AND DIDN'T I SEE SOME PRETTY MUSHROOMS IN LA NAAN?
OOH! LET'S GO! LET'S GO!

SO, YOU HAVEN'T SEEN HER?
NO, I HAVEN'T, BUT I'LL ORDER A SEARCH.
IF SHE WERE IN LA NAAN...
....
...I'M SURE SHE'D HAVE COME TO SEE ME.
WOULDN'T SHE?

スタ
スタ
スタ

YOU NEVER KNOW WITH ISHTAR.

Touchy, touchy...
That's why I don't date princes. Too much drama.

JILL! KRAI!
SORRY, CAPTAIN!!

EXCUSE ME, BUT IS LADY RAMIA AROUND?
NO, SHE'S OFF AT A SPA.
SHE HAD A BIT OF A... BREAK-DOWN AFTER VORD LEFT.
SHE GOT INTO A FIGHT WITH SEILIEZ AND WENT AWAY TO COOL OFF A LITTLE.

A BREAK-DOWN AFTER PRINCE VORD LEFT, EH?
HE HARDLY SEEMS WORTH IT.
....
VORD LEAVING LA NAAN TO FOLLOW ISHTAR TO THE CAPITAL...
...PROBABLY UPSET LADY RAMIA'S PLANS.
BUT SOMETHING'S CHANGED IF SEILIEZ CAN GET TO HER LIKE THAT.
WELL, IF ISHTAR ISN'T HERE, WHERE IS SHE?

Near Ci Xeneth Castle

DARRES SAID HE WOULD RETURN TO LA NAAN TO LOOK FOR ISHTAR THERE.
AND I SAID I'D LOOK UP NORTH BY MYSELF. I HAD TO OPEN MY BIG MOUTH...
SO THIS IS CI XENETH? NICE PLACE.
EVERYONE SEEMS HAPPY.

THEY'RE ALL GOING ABOUT THEIR DAILY LIVES CHEERFULLY AND FREE OF STRESS.

...EXACTLY THE OPPOSITE OF THE WAY THEY'D BE ACTING IF ISHTAR HAD PASSED THROUGH HERE.

NOT THAT THEIR MONARCH, LORD JENED, IS MUCH BETTER.
I HEAR HE'S OPENLY THREATENED TO MURDER ANY CANDIDATE FOR ISHTAR'S HAND...
...OR EVEN ISHTAR HERSELF.

SIR KNIGHT, YOU MUST HELP US!
LAST NIGHT THE MONSTERS TOOK EIGHT MORE OF OUR PEOPLE!
PLEASE SEND CAPTAIN ILLSAIDE! WE'RE DESPERATE!
THEY ATTACKED MY VILLAGE TOO!
WE NEED HELP!

SHUT UP AND MOVE ALONG!

YOU KNOW DAMN WELL THAT CAPTAIN ILLSAIDE ONLY HUNTS MONSTERS ON LORD JENED'S ORDERS!

ONE MORE WORD AND I'LL THROW YOU IN THE STOCKS!

YOU HEAR ME?! NOW GET LOST!!

MONSTERS? WHAT THE HELL?

THERE SHOULDN'T BE ANY MONSTERS THIS FAR NORTH.

BESIDES, MOST MONSTERS I'VE HUNTED ARE SKITTISH. THEY GO OUT OF THE WAY TO AVOID HUMAN SETTLEMENTS.
MUST BE THE SMELL.
DIDN'T YOU HEAR US? MOVE! WAIT A MINUTE... YOU'RE NOT FROM AROUND HERE, ARE YOU?

AND THAT'S THE FIRST GOOD NEWS I'VE HEARD ALL DAY.

DON'T YOU THINK, DADDY?

THEY'RE SIMILAR ONLY IN THE WAY THEY LOOK.
DU SEEMS MUCH SMARTER THAN THAT IDIOTIC COUSIN OF YOURS.

LISTEN, DU...

...NO MATTER WHAT, JUST INSIST THAT YOU'RE NOT ME. WHICH SHOULDN'T BE TOO TOUGH...
...SINCE YOU REALLY AREN'T ME. ARE YOU?
IF THAT DOESN'T WORK...
...JUST COUGH UP A HAIRBALL AND MAKE YOUR GETAWAY WHILE THEY'RE STILL IN SHOCK!
And grab some bread or something, I'm starved.
NO, THANKFULLY I'M NOT YOU, ISHTAR. BUT JUST ONCE, I WISH YOU COULD BE ME...BEING YOU...

ILLSAIDE ...
YOU'VE NEVER MET LADY ISHTAR, HAVE YOU?
NO, I HAVEN'T.
BUT I'VE HEARD SHE'S QUITE BEAUTIFUL.
BEAUTIFUL ...

...THAT YOUR NEW GIRLFRIEND IS A COMPLETE JEWEL.

I CAN SEE WHY ISHTAR LIKES FALAN. SHE MAY NOT BE THE PRETTIEST GIRL OUT THERE, BUT I'D BITE HER.

WHY IS FALAN SO OBSESSED WITH HOW PRETTY ISHTAR IS? IS SHE JEALOUS?

OR IS THIS JUST HER WAY OF COMPLI-MENTING ME IN FRONT OF ILLSAIDE?

THAT'S NONSENSE.

COUGH!
I'LL HEAR NO MORE OF THIS.
YOU'RE THE MOST BEAUTIFUL GIRL IN PHELIOSTA. THAT WRETCHED ISHTAR DOESN'T EVEN COPARE.
EXCUSE ME!
Hair-balls... ya know?
YOU REALLY DO LOOK LIKE ISHTAR.

IF YOU ONLY HAD HER FIGURE...
I'D THINK YOU TWO WERE TWINS!
YOU'RE RIGHT. MS. DU DOES LOOK LIKE ISHTAR.
A BIT MORE BOYISH, PERHAPS.
I SHOULD GET OUT OF HERE.
ILLSAIDE...

...CAN I TALK TO DU IN PRIVATE?
GIRL TALK. YOU UNDER-STAND... RIGHT?

OF COURSE.
WHATEVER YOU WISH, YOUR HIGHNESS.
LOOK, GUYS, I ALREADY TOLD YOU EVERY-THING.
I'M LOOKING FOR A GIRL.
HER NAME'S ISHTAR, BUT SHE MIGHT BE CALLING HERSELF DUZELL.
SHE'S GOT BLACK HAIR AND GREEN EYES. SHE'S ABOUT 16 YEARS OLD, VERY PRETTY, AND TROUBLE FOLLOWS HER AROUND LIKE A LITTER OF LOVE-STARVED KITTENS.

THAT SOUNDS LIKE...
THEM?
YOU KNOW WHERE THEY ARE? I MEAN, WHERE SHE IS?
HE COULDN'T BE TALKING ABOUT THEM, COULD HE?
WHY ARE YOU LOOKING FOR THIS GIRL?
ARE YOU RELATED?
RELATED?

I'D LIKE TO SAY I'M HER FIANCÉE, BUT...
...FOR NOW...
I'M HER BROTHER.
BROTHER?!
CAN YOU FIGHT LIKE DU? IS YOUR MAGIC AS GOOD AS ISHTA'S?
MAGIC? WELL, I WOULD HOPE SO!
ISHTAR'S NOT ONE TO GO AROUND CASTING DANGEROUS SPELLS, BUT IN HER HANDS, EVEN A GOOD LUCK CHARM IS DANGEROUS.
WHAT'S SHE UP TO? AND WHY ARE THESE GUARDS SO STIRRED UP?

タッ
タッ
タッ
I WONDER WHAT DARRES IS DOING NOW?

KNOWING HIM, HE'S PROBABLY DISCUSSING SPANKING TECHNIQUES WITH THE DUNGEON MASTER.
HE'S GOT TO BE STRESSING OUT! HIS HAIR IS PROBABLY TURNING WHITE!
IF I KEEP THIS UP, HE'LL LOOK JUST LIKE THE OLD FART!
I DON'T WANT THAT...

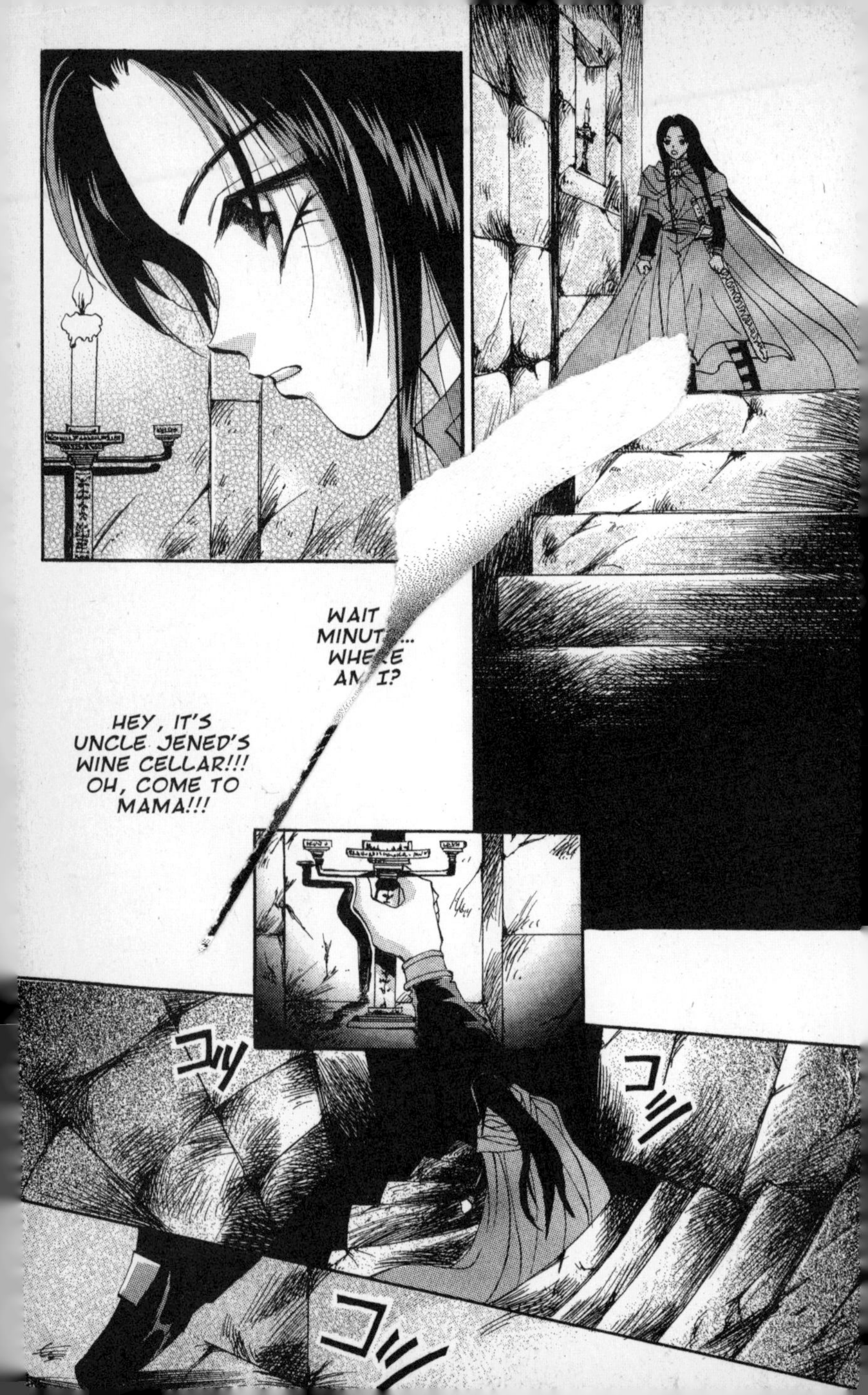
WAIT MINUTE... WHERE AM I?
HEY, IT'S UNCLE JENED'S WINE CELLAR!!! OH, COME TO MAMA!!!
コツ
コツ
コツ

......?!
SHRIEK

......?!
WHAT ARE YOU DOING DOWN HERE?
UH...
ROY! YOU SCARED THE CRAP OUT OF ME!

ROY, WHAT ARE YOU DOING HERE?
YOU MEAN THIS ISN'T THE BATHROOM?! THE GUARD SAID IT WAS THE EIGHTH DOOR ON THE RIGHT. DID I MISCOUNT?
Well, I'll be... um, going now. Heh heh...
WANT TO SEE?
UH... SURE?
WE'VE BEEN WORKING ON THIS FOR YEARS.

NEARLY A DECADE OF GATHERING THE MOST EXOTIC OF INGREDIENTS...
...JUST TO MAKE RUELLES FOR LORD JENED.
RUELLES?
PLEASE, MAKE YOURSELF AT HOME.

PHELIOS MUST HAVE PASSED ON SOME TWISTED GENES...
I MEAN...
...THE MEN IN THIS FAMILY ARE PRETTIER THAN THE WOMEN.

POOR GIRL... FOREVER IN ISHTAR'S SHADOW.
YOU'RE DISMISSED.
BUT, PRINCESS ...
IT'S ALL RIGHT.

ゾロ ゾロ
パタン
I'M SORRY. THAT WAS RUDE OF ME.

I...
I'M JUST...
...A LITTLE JEALOUS THAT ILLSAIDE PICKED YOU. HOW'D HE POP THE QUESTION?
HUH?
POP THE QUESTION?
DOES SHE MEAN...?

"THANK YOU."
"I'M NOT VERY GOOD AT THIS KIND OF THING, SO I DON'T REALLY KNOW WHAT TO SAY. I DIDN'T EXPECT IT TO BE SO EASY."
"DU, WHATEVER HAPPENS, I JUST WANT YOU TO KNOW..."
"...I'D GIVE MY LIFE TO PROTECT YOU."

THAT BASTARD!
HE'S PLAYING BOTH OF US!!
OH NO, IT'S NOT LIKE THAT!
I...I LOVE HIM, BUT HE DOESN'T LOVE ME.
HE TOLD ME THAT OVER A YEAR AGO.
A YEAR AGO?

ABOUT A MONTH AFTER HE CAME BACK FROM THE MERARIM CAMPAIGN...
...ILLSAIDE TOLD ME HE COULDN'T MARRY ME.
HE SAID HE'D FALLEN IN LOVE WITH A BEAUTIFUL WOMAN.

YOU'RE NOT ISHTAR, BUT-- OUCH!-- YOU'RE SO MUCH LIKE HER.
I FEEL LIKE I'VE KNOWN YOU FOR YEARS.
I FEEL LIKE I CAN TRUST YOU.
"...I LIKE FALAN. SHE'S REALLY SWEET."

THIS IS JUST WONDERFUL !!
I THOUGHT I WOULD HAVE TO SEND HER TO A CONVENT, BUT HEY, THIS WORKS TOO!
NOW, MAYBE FALAN CAN FINALLY GET OVER YOU! SHE KEEPS ME UP AT NIGHT, CHATTERING ON ABOUT HOW SHE'LL DIE WITHOUT YOU.
AND I MUST SAY, YOU SURE KNOW HOW TO CHOOSE 'EM. NICE RACK, NICE ASS. YOU WILL, OF COURSE, "TRY HER ON" BEFORE PURCHASING, WON'T YOU?

くす
くす
くす
ILLSAIDE...
ILLSAIDE...

YOU KNOW WHAT THE PEOPLE SAY ABOUT YOU?
I'VE HEARD THEM SAY YOU'RE A HOLY WARRIOR!
OR EVEN THE REINCARNATION OF PHELIOS HIMSERLF!
YOU'RE THE MOST POPULAR KNIGHT IN CI XENETH.
EVEN MORE POPULAR THAN MY FATHER!

DADDY GIVES YOU SO MUCH ATTENTION, ILLSAIDE.
I'M ALMOST JEALOUS!
ILLSAIDE, I ASKED...
...MY FATHER SOMETHING.
HE
...IF THE MAN WAS WORTHY OF ME...
...MY HUSBAND WOULDN'T HAVE TO BE A DESCENDANT OF PHELIOS.

ILLSAIDE...
YOU'RE DISMISSED. AND GIVE THAT GORGEOUS GIRL'S ASS A SQUEEZE FOR ME!

THIS HAS BEEN ONE VERY STRANGE NIGHT.
ILLSAIDE SEEMS NICE ENOUGH...
...BUT THE GUY HAS THE PERSONALITY OF A RADISH.
AS FOR FALAN...

WELL, SHE'S TASTY. BUT SHE'S NOT PHELIOS' REINCARNATION.

WHICH LEAVES HER FATHER, LORD JENED.

COULD HE BE PHELIOS?

SOMEHOW I DOUBT IT...

トントン

トントン

ABOUT BLOODY TIME...

WHERE HAVE YOU BEEN?!

PRINCE VORD!!
YOUR HIGHNESS!! WHAT THE HELL ARE YOU DOING HERE?! YOU'VE WORRIED US HALF TO DEATH!

THIS IS BAD...
VERY BAD...
.........!!

SO IF YOU NEED A LILKE'S SOUL TO MAKE A RING OF TRANSPOR-TATION...
...WHAT'S IT TAKE TO MAKE A SWORD LIKE SIDIA?
A GOOD QUESTION. FOR A RUELLE LIKE THAT, YOU'D NEED HOLY MAGIC...
...AND THE SOULS OF VAMPIRES. LOTS OF THEM.
VAMPIRE SOULS?! IN SIDIA?!
YES. SIDIA WAS CREATED TO DESTROY DUZELL. ITS FORGING REQUIRED...
を
...THE SOULS OF MANY VAMPIRES FROM DUZELL'S CLAN.

A POWERFUL CREATURE LIKE A VAMPIRE CAN ONLY BE DEFEATED...
...BY A RUELLE WITH GREATER MAGICAL ENERGY...
AND A HOLY SPELL THAT'S AT LEAST AS POWERFUL AS THE RUELLE.
IN DUZELL'S CASE, THE ENERGY REQUIRED WAS INCREDIBLE.
THAT IS WHY YOUR ANCESTORS MATED WITH THESE MONSTERS.

MY ANCESTORS DID WHAT?!
A MONSTER'S LOOSE!
DAMMIT, MEN! STAND YOUR GROUND!!

A MONSTER?!
DUZIE!!
......

WHY DIDN'T YOU KILL HER?
KILL HER?
THAT WOULD RUIN IT.
NO, WE HAVE SOMETHING MUCH MORE SPECTACULAR PLANNED FOR HER.
DON'T WE ISHTAR?

I CAN SEE IT IN YOUR EYES.
YOU MAY BE KNOWN AS ISHTAR NOW, BUT YOUR SOUL IS THAT OF PHELIOS!

吸血遊戯
シー・ゼネス
東領篇
Act.7

パラ
パラ
SO, THE VAMPIRE'S PROPHECY IS TRUE. PHELIOS HAS RETURNED AND IS IN OUR PRESENCE. NOT THAT HE EVEN REALIZES IT.
POOR HUMANS.
WHEN YOUR SOULS ARE REBORN, YOUR PAST LIVES ARE LEFT BEHIND. A WHOLE LIFE LIVED WITHOUT SO MUCH AS A SOUVENIR.

NO MEMORY...
PHYSICAL TRAITS...
TALENTS...
EVEN YOUR PERSONALITY IS TOSSED ASIDE FOR SOMETHING NEW.
DUZELL MAY HAVE PREDICTED PHELIOS' REBIRTH.
BUT EVEN HE WOULD HAVE A HELL OF A TIME SPOTTING HIM.
AND UNLIKE A VAMPIRE, I DON'T HAVE THE BENEFIT OF USING BLOOD AS A MEANS OF IDENTIFICA-TION.
HOWEVER, ACCORDING TO DUZELL'S PROPHECY, PHELIOS WILL BE REBORN BACK INTO THE SAME BLOODLINE.
THAT MEANS THERE ARE ONLY A HANDFUL OF PEOPLE IT COULD BE. AND I'VE MET MOST OF THEM. A HOG WOULD BE A WORTHIER REINCARNATION.

NO, IT'S REASONABLE TO ASSUME THAT THE NEW PHELIOS WILL SHARE AT LEAST A FEW TRAITS WITH THE OLD ONE.
EVEN IF THEY AREN'T AS OBVIOUS AS MEMORY, APPEARANCE, TALENT OR PERSONALITY.
PERHAPS IT IS SOME-THING MORE GENERAL, LESS TANGIBLE...

SOMETHING LIKE HIS WILL OR SPIRIT...
I'VE BEEN WATCHING PHELIOS' SORRY FAMILY FOR DECADES...
AND THIS BRATTY PRINCESS MUST BE THE ONE.

AFTER ALL...
THEIR RESPONSES ARE EXACTLY THE SAME!
HUH?!
WHERE AM I?

MY WORKSHOP IN THE BASEMENT.
BUT...
...THERE'S A BIG COMMOTION UPSTAIRS. BANDITS, MAYBE?
WHY DON'T YOU CHECK IT OUT?
ダッ

DU, ARE YOU ALL RIGHT?
I'M FINE! WHERE HAVE YOU BEEN?
YOU'RE MISSING ALL THE EXCITEMENT!

UH...I WAS--
I'VE HAD QUITE A NIGHT! NO THANKS TO YOU, I MIGHT ADD!
FIRST, YOU MAKE ME WEAR A DRESS SO I CAN GO OUT WITH MY "BOYFRIEND," THEN FALAN DECIDES TO CONFIDE IN ME...
THEN MONSTERS POP UP EVERY-WHERE...
JUST AS VORD COMES POUNDING AT MY DOOR ASKING ME--
VORD? DO I KNOW HIM?
DON'T BE AN IDIOT!
HE'S THE GIANT THAT FOLLOWED YOU HOME FROM LA NAAN!
Oh, that Vord.

WHAT'S HE DOING HERE?
LOOKING FOR YOU! WHAT ELSE WOULD HE BE DOING?!

....

OH NO!
WE CAN'T RUN INTO VORD NOW!
AS FAR AS HE KNOWS, YOU'RE MY CAT!
IF HE SEES YOU IN HUMAN FORM I'M SURE HE'LL START PUTTING TWO AND TWO TOGETHER AND...
Our story is falling apart...

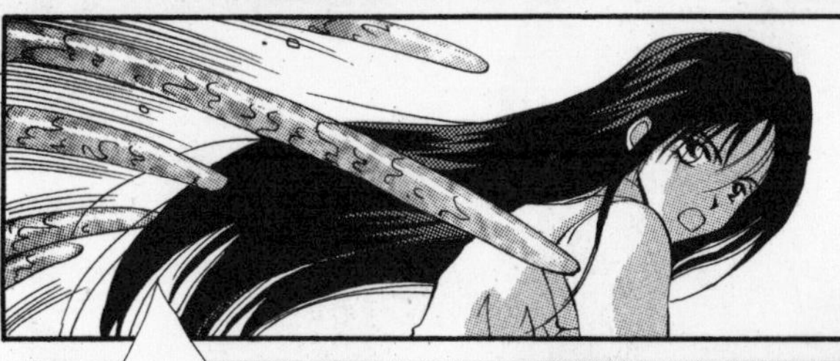
PRINCESS, THIS IS ALL VERY INTEREST-ING.

AND I WANT TO TALK TO YOU ABOUT IT. REALLY, I DO.

BUT MAY I PLEASE TAKE CARE OF THIS OVERGROWN SLUG FIRST?!!

HOLY MAGIC...
BUT THAT MEANS...
CAPTAIN!

......!
HAS ANYONE FOUND THIS BEAST'S BODY?
WHAT THE HELL?!

ズキッ
IT TORE THROUGH THE FLOOR...
...SPREADING ITS TENTACLES INTO THE CASTLE FROM BELOW.
すッ
PLEASE PROTECT THE PRINCESS.
ILLSAIDE!

I DON'T GET IT. IS ILLSAIDE REALLY IN LOVE WITH FALAN?
THE WAY HE'S BEEN ACTING COULDN'T BE... COULD IT?
....
ISHTAR?
YOU ARE ISHTAR...
RIGHT?
......

......
YOU GOT ME.
YOU ALWAYS WERE A SMART ONE. C'MON, GIVE YOUR COUSIN A HUG!

サラッ

"KISS OF THE ANGELS," A WISE CHOICE OF SPELL...

NOT BAD...
LITTLE PUNK'S BETTER THAN I GAVE HIM CREDIT FOR.

I DIDN'T EVEN RECOGNIZE THAT LAST SPELL...

THE GUY'S PROBABLY BEEN PRACTICING MAGIC SINCE HE WAS IN DIAPERS.
AND HE'S NOT A PRINCE, SO WHO TAUGHT HIM?

ILLSAIDE, WELL DONE, MY BOY!
なでなで

LORD JENED...
!

JENED?
INTERESTING.
SO, THAT'S THE BIG MAN...
ベタ
ベタ
DOESN'T LOOK LIKE MUCH.
ベタ
ベタ
WHEW! THAT WAS ONE POWERFUL SPELL!
LORD JENED TAUGHT THAT BOY WELL.
HE SURE HAS! I MEAN...
...THE CAPTAIN... IS...UH, QUITE SKILLED.

I'LL SAY! I THOUGHT THE ROYAL FAMILY KEPT THEIR HOLY MAGIC UNDER LOCK AND KEY! WELL, YOU LEARN SOMETHING NEW EVERY DAY.
ONE MYSTERY'S SOLVED, BUT IT HAS PRESENTED US WITH A NEW ONE. SPECIFICALLY, WHAT'S GOING ON BETWEEN THOSE TWO?
ILLSAIDE'S GOOD-LOOKING.
ALMOST AS HANDSOME AS SHARLEN.

SPEAK OF THE DEVIL... SHARLEN?!
NO, IT CAN'T BE!
HE'S MUCH TOO OLD...
....

I JUS'
CAIN'T
DO THIS
ALONE...

WHY'D YOU TELL HER THAT? THE LAST THING WE NEED IS HER STICKING HER NECK IN OUR BUSINESS!
I DIDN'T TELL HER, SHE GUESSED. I FIGURED WE MIGHT AS WELL COME CLEAN.
......
I THOUGHT YOU ONLY SAW HER ONCE A YEAR!
NO, THAT'S MY UNCLE.
I SEE FALAN ALL THE TIME!
WE HANG OUT AT LEAST ONCE A MONTH.
WE'LL GET TOGETHER, PAINT OUR NAILS, GOSSIP ABOUT GUYS...
WHY DIDN'T YOU TELL ME?!

YOU TWO LOOK SO MUCH ALIKE-- IT'S INCREDIBLE!
DID YOU MEET EACH OTHER IN CI XENETH?
UH...YEAH, WE DID! WEIRD,HUH?!
GOOD ONE, ISHTA. ALWAYS THINKING ONE STEP AHEAD...
SO WHY ARE YOU HERE? NOT THAT I'M NOT GLAD TO SEE YOU...
IT'S...UH... A SECRET MISSION.
REALLY? HOW COOL! I GUESS I WON'T SAY ANYTHING TO DADDY, THEN.

SO WHAT'S THE MISSION ABOUT?
I MEAN, I CAN'T SAY THAT I'M LOOKING FOR OUR GREAT-GRANDFATHER'S REINCARNATION WITH THE VAMPIRE KING DUZELL WHO IS REALLY A BABY KYAWL DISGUISED AS ME...NOW. CAN I?
FALAN, IT'S A SECRET MISSION.
LET'S JUST SAY...
THAT I'M REALLY INTO RUELLES RIGHT NOW.
AND SINCE YOUR FATHER IS AN EXPERT ON THEM...
RUELLES?
I HATE THOSE THINGS! I WISH HE'D NEVER HEARD OF THEM!
WHY?

THEY'RE ALL DADDY TALKS ABOUT ANYMORE!
AND THEY CAUSE NOTHING BUT SUFFERING! THE MERARIM WAR STARTED OVER RUELLES!
THAT'S RIDICULOUS. THERE ISN'T A RUELLE POWERFUL ENOUGH TO START A WAR.
NOT YET THERE ISN'T! BUT MERARIM FACES THE OCEAN, AND THAT OCEAN IS FULL OF UNUSUAL CREATURES. MY FATHER WANTED THOSE MONSTERS TO MAKE MORE RUELLES...
UNUSUAL MONSTERS... HE WANTED THEIR SOULS.
...BUT THE MERARIMIANS REFUSED!
THEY WOULDN'T LET MY FATHER'S MEN ENTER THE OCEAN.

THEY CLAIMED THAT 20 YEARS AGO...
...MY FATHER DID THE SAME THING...
...AND THAT, SOMEHOW, THE OCEAN HAS NEVER BEEN THE SAME SINCE.
IT WAS AS IF THE WATERS WERE CURSED. THE FISH BECAME SCARCE...
AND THE SONS OF MERARIM VANISHED AT SEA!
HE PLACED A CURSE ON THE WHOLE OCEAN?
HE SWEARS HE DIDN'T, AND HE WAS WILLING TO GO TO WAR TO PROVE IT.
HE WAS WILLING TO RISK THE LIVES OF MEN.
ILLSAIDE WAS HURT.
ALL FOR SOME STUPID RUELLES!
I'M SORRY, FALAN. I'M SORRY.
ILLSAIDE WAS HURT?

......
カツ
カツ

I ALWAYS KNEW...
...THERE WAS SOMETHING...
...VERY STRANGE ABOUT YOU, BOY.
OH, YES...
HOWEVER, EVEN I NEVER WOULD HAVE GUESSED WHAT IT WAS.
THEN AGAIN, IT DOES SEEM LIKE HIS STYLE.

WITH ALL LORD JENED'S INTEREST IN MONSTERS...
...IT SEEMS ONLY NATURAL THAT HE WOULD WANT ONE...
...LEADING HIS ARMY.
YOU'RE A HALF-BREED. AREN'T YOU, BOY?
AREN'T YOU?
TO BE CONTINUED IN VOLUME 6

じろじろ
I'M NOT SURE SIR KELD WILL ALLOW HIM INTO THE CASTLE...
...MUCH LESS INTO THE ROYAL GUARD! HA HA HA!
THAT ARROGANT PIECE OF--
OKAY, GOTTA CALM DOWN.
I'M SORRY. ALL MY DRESS CLOAKS ARE IN THE WASH.
EXCUSE ME...
BUT I'D LIKE YOU TO THINK ABOUT HOW PAINFUL IT WILL BE TO RIDE A HORSE...
!!
........!

...ONCE MY MACE HAS CONNECTED WITH YOUR SCROTUM. YOU SPEAK TO HIM LIKE THAT AGAIN, AND YOU WON'T HAVE TO *THINK* ABOUT IT ANYMORE.
SELEN?!
OH NO, CAPTAIN!
WHAT I MEANT WAS, UH... OH, WHAT'S THAT OVER THERE?!
すたこらさっさ

SELEN, YOU DON'T HAVE TO DO THIS I DON'T HAVE TO BE A ROYAL GUARD--
OKAY...
DON'T WORRY. THE ONLY PERSON WHO MATTERS AROUND HERE IS SIR KELD.
AS LONG AS HE LIKES YOU, YOU HAVE NOTHING TO WORRY ABOUT.
AND HE'LL LIKE YOU. TRUST ME.
...WAIT FOR ME HERE.
I'LL BE BACK IN A MINUTE!
....

WHY CAN'T I JUST...
I DON'T KNOW IF I EVEN WANT TO BE A ROYAL GUARD.
...STAY WITH SELEN FOREVER?
WHY DO THINGS HAVE TO CHANGE?

Hi! ♡
......
ABSOLUTELY NOT!
NO WAY!
THIS IS A CASTLE, NOT AN ORPHANAGE!
THAT BOY IS A THIEF!

HE IS AN ORPHAN, FIGHTING TO STAY ALIVE!
HE'S BRAVE, SIR KELD! AND HE'S ABSOLUTELY BRILLIANT WITH A SWORD! HE'S WORTH A DOZEN OF YOUR KNIGHTS! YOU KNOW THAT!!
......
WHAT DO YOU THINK?
SELEN, I'M AFRAID I CAN'T ALLOW--
I DON'T KNOW, SIR...
......
I DON'T BELIEVE THIS!

SIR KELD!
CAPTAIN SELEN!
IT'S AN EMERGENCY!
LADY ISHTAR IS MISSING AGAIN!

HAVE SOME SOUP!
SOUP?
OH, I GET IT. IT'S A GAME...
WHY, THANK YOU! I'D LOVE SOME SOUP.
HAVE SOME MORE!
WHOA!
TEE HEE HEE!
WHAT A LITTLE BRAT!

HEY!
GET BACK HERE!
GOTCHA!
!

WHAT THE HELL? WHAT ARE THOSE THINGS?!
HANG ON TIGHT, KID!

SOMETHING TELLS ME THESE AREN'T YOUR BABY-SITTERS!

LADY ISHTAR!
LADY ISHTAR!!
ザァ
ザァァァァ

DARRES!!
ピクッ
ハァ
ハァ
SELEN, WHAT THE HELL JUST HAPPENED?
ALL THESE MONSTERS...
...JUST CAME OUT OF THE FOUNTAIN!
And they weren't trying to pick up all the pennies.

ONE OF THE LEGSARAM CHARMS IS BROKEN.
DARRES!
!
Holding on for dear life.
DARRES?

LADY ISHTAR!!

SHE'S NOTHING LIKE SELEN.
THEY'RE LIKE NIGHT AND DAY. SELEN'S THE SUN, AND ISHTAR'S THE MOON...
Appropriate, considering she mooned me this morning.
I DON'T SEE THE RESEMBLANCE.
I SAW IT SOON ENOUGH...
LADY ISHTAR, THIS IS DARRES. HE'S GOING TO BE YOUR NEW BODYGUARD.

HELLO!

Postscript

VAMPIRE GAME

Next issue...

By now it's fairly clear that if you're going to call Ci Xeneth home, you'd better be packing Prozac. The weather's lousy, the crime rate is high, and the king is taking advice from a psychotic. Then there are the monsters. Contrary to popular belief, monsters aren't unreasonable. They usually don't tear people in half unless they're provoked, so the general rule is that you never want to make a monster mad. And using a bunch of their brethren to craft Ruelles tends to tick them off. Lord Jened should know better, and when an army of monsters attacks his castle, perhaps he'll learn his lesson. He won't get much help from Ishtar and Duzell. They've had it with Ci Xeneth and are ready to hit the road, after Duzie downs a few drops of Jened juice, of course. And if the monsters can make that any easier, so much the better...

ALSO AVAILABLE FROM TOKYOPOP®

REBOUND
REMOTE
RISING STARS OF MANGA
SABER MARIONETTE J
SAILOR MOON
SAINT TAIL
SAMURAI DEEPER KYO
SAMURAI GIRL REAL BOUT HIGH SCHOOL
SCRYED
SEIKAI TRILOGY, THE CREST OF THE STARS
SGT. FROG
SHAOLIN SISTERS
SHIRAHIME-SYO: SNOW GODDESS TALES
SHUTTERBOX
SKULL MAN, THE
SNOW DROP
SORCERER HUNTERS
STONE
SUIKODEN III
SUKI
TOKYO BABYLON
TOKYO MEW MEW
UNDER THE GLASS MOON
VAMPIRE GAME
VISION OF ESCAFLOWNE, THE
WILD ACT
WISH
WORLD OF HARTZ
X-DAY
ZODIAC P.I.

NOVELS

KARMA CLUB
SAILOR MOON

ART BOOKS

CARDCAPTOR SAKURA
CLAMP NORTHSIDE
CLAMP SOUTHSIDE
MAGIC KNIGHT RAYEARTH
PEACH: MIWA UEDA ILLUSTRATIONS

ANIME GUIDES

COWBOY BEBOP ANIME GUIDES
GUNDAM TECHNICAL MANUALS
SAILOR MOON SCOUT GUIDES

TOKYOPOP KIDS

STRAY SHEEP

CINE-MANGA™

ASTRO BOY
CARDCAPTORS
DUEL MASTERS
FAIRLY ODDPARENTS, THE
FINDING NEMO
G.I. JOE SPY TROOPS
JACKIE CHAN ADVENTURES
JIMMY NEUTRON BOY GENIUS, THE ADVENTURES OF
KIM POSSIBLE
LILO & STITCH
LIZZIE MCGUIRE
LIZZIE MCGUIRE: THE MOVIE
MALCOLM IN THE MIDDLE
POWER RANGERS: NINJA STORM
SHREK 2
SPONGEBOB SQUAREPANTS
SPY KIDS 2
SPY KIDS 3-D: GAME OVER
TEENAGE MUTANT NINJA TURTLES
THAT'S SO RAVEN
TRANSFORMERS: ARMADA
TRANSFORMERS: ENERGON

For more information visit www.TOKYOPOP.com

01.09.04T

STOP!

This is the back of the book. You wouldn't want to spoil a great ending!

This book is printed "manga-style," in the authentic Japanese right-to-left format. Since none of the artwork has been flipped or altered, readers get to experience the story just as the creator intended. You've been asking for it, so TOKYOPOP® delivered: authentic, hot-off-the-press, and far more fun!

DIRECTIONS

If this is your first time reading manga-style, here's a quick guide to help you understand how it works.

It's easy... just start in the top right panel and follow the numbers. Have fun, and look for more 100% authentic manga from TOKYOPOP®!